HUMANS IN SPACE

BIG IDEAS: LOW INTERMEDIATE

MARTIN HAJOVSKY

WAYZGOOSE PRESS

CONTENTS

SUPPLEMENTARY MATERIALS

For *Big Ideas* downloadable learning tools for students and teachers, go to

http://wayzgoosepress.com/books/readers-choicevariety-pack-big-ideas-intermediate/

INTRODUCTION

When you read an article or story, you have a conversation. The writer shares information, experiences, and ideas – but you, the reader, have your own ideas. When you read, you compare your experience and knowledge with the writer's ideas. Then you make decisions. Do you agree with the writer? Can you use the information to be healthier or more successful in your job, for example? Do you feel like the writer understands your life? Or do you learn about someone with a different point of view?

Because reading is a conversation, every reader experiences a text differently. When you read something interesting, you often want to talk about it. You want to share a similar experience, or you may want to argue. Maybe your friend understands the text in a different way. When you listen to your friend, you have a third set of ideas and experiences to compare to your own world view.

Big Ideas is designed to start interesting conversations between readers and writers, but also between readers and other readers. In this book about humans in space, you'll learn the story of humans leaving Earth for the first time. The articles detail the work of astronauts, engineers, and scientists who worked on large and small projects to find out more about the Moon and our nearest neighboring planet, Mars. Many of their plans failed. Sometimes people died. However, the adventure of space never stopped, and it is not likely to stop in the future. There are always new and interesting questions to explore. What is it like to live in space? Will we ever live on Mars?

While you learn about space exploration, *Big Ideas* is also helping you develop language skills. Because our focus is on providing a positive reading experience, more than 90 percent of the words in this book are among the most common 2000 words in the English language. These are called "high-frequency words." High frequency words appear over and over again in speaking and writing.

You might think it will be easy to learn high frequency words, and it is true that many words are easy. Content words such as *tree, house, eat, drink*, and *blue* put a picture in your mind. They represent things you can see and name. They often have one meaning, and you can translate them easily.

However, many high frequency words change their meaning when they partner with other words in collocations. *Stay* is an example. When we say, *I stayed home yesterday*, then *stay* has a different meaning from *Let's try to stay awake all night* or *Stay away from the cookies. I'm saving them for the party*. This flexibility shows that *stay* does not just have one meaning. It adapts to the words around it.

Fortunately, there is a method to learn the different meanings of collocations: read a lot. When you read, you see words in different combinations, and you learn their meanings. This can happen naturally, but it will happen faster if you pay attention to words in groups. When you notice and highlight or copy word combinations, you can learn the different meanings.

You can also learn the grammar that goes with a vocabulary word. For example, you might see *educate* as a verb in *educate children, education* as a noun in *a college education,* and *educational* as an adjective in *an educational experience*. You will also notice that some verbs are usually followed by a preposition, such as *talk about* or *talk to*, while others are followed by a noun, as in *hear a bird*. These grammatical details are hard to hear in spoken English, but they are easy to see in a written text. At the back of the book, we have provided a tool for developing language awareness in this way.

While vocabulary has a strong relationship with grammar, grammar has a strong relationship with sentences. In order to give you a positive reading experience, we have used easy-to-read sentences. We use grammar from low and intermediate levels, and we reduce synonyms and idioms. Our goal is to keep the big ideas about space, but present them in simple language.

A NOTE ON CAPITALIZATION AND PUNCTUATION

In these stories about space exploration, you will read about space programs and missions as well as space stations, space ships, lunar modules, and other vehicles you probably don't read about very often. Punctuation can help you understand what you are reading about, so we would like to let you know about the system of capitalization and italics that we used in this book.

We followed the style guide of the National Aeronautics and Space Administration (NASA) of the United States, which can be found on their website. Further examples can be found on the website of the National Aeronautics and Space Museum.

Some of the conventions include:

- Earth is capitalized (when it refers to our planet) as well as Moon and Sun when they refer to the ones closest to our Earth. So, we write **I can see the Moon at night**, but **The planet Jupiter has more than 60 moons**.
- Terms such as the **solar system** and the **universe** are not capitalized.

- Names of vehicles that orbit (go around planets and moons) are italicized, such as *Discovery*.
- Lunar module and command module names are italicized, such as *Eagle* and *Odyssey*.
- "Personal" names for spacecraft are italicized, but not company brand names and numbers. So, the Space Shuttle is not italicized, but the Space Shuttle *Challenger* is.
- Probes and robotic spacecraft (for example, Voyager or Cassini), that never carry people, are not italicized. Rovers, such as the Mars rover Curiosity, are also not italicized.
- The names of missions (that is, programs) are not italicized. However, manned spacecraft are italicized. Remember that Apollo 13 is the name of a program; but *Apollo 13* is also the name of a spacecraft. The italics will help you figure out quickly which one you are reading about.
- Space stations, like Skylab, have people, but they are not vehicles—so they are not italicized.
- Dates for decades are written without an apostrophe: **1960s**, and not **1960's**.
- Dates for individual days are written in the format day-month-year; so, 11 April 1969 and not April 11, 1969. This is not common in American English in general, but is more common in British English as well as other systems throughout the world. When scientists communicate with each other, being clear and accurate is very important, so they agree on what systems to use that everybody can easily understand.

LEAVING EARTH

This picture of the Earth rising over the Moon was taken by Apollo 8 command module pilot William Anders in December 1968. This was the first time any human had seen the Earth from this distance. (Photo credit: NASA)

There is a first time for everything. The first people to climb Mount Everest were Edmund Hillary and Tenzing Norgay. The first person to fly in an airplane was Orville Wright. The first person to travel faster than sound was Chuck Yeager. Years later, many other people have done the same things, but we remember the first person to achieve a remarkable goal.

Since 1957, there have been many firsts in space exploration. One person reaches a goal. The next person goes further. Each achievement in space exploration builds on the one before. However, we remember the first time, because gives us confidence to achieve even more in the future.

HUMANS ON THE MOVE

Human beings now travel and live in space. This is so common that we sometimes forget that space travel is new. Only a little over a hundred years ago, on 17 December 1903, the Wright Brothers flew the first airplane at Kitty Hawk, North Carolina. Orville and Wilbur Wright, a pair of bicycle mechanics, were the first people to design a machine that would allow people to control the skies.

Think about what that means. Human beings have been alive on this planet for millions of years. At some point, nobody knows why, some people started to move. Some moved very far away. Over time, humans kept moving until they covered this entire planet. What do we learn from this? One lesson is that humans like to explore. Humans want to go over the next hill. Then we want to know what is over the one after that, and the one after that. As we explore, we learn, we change, and we take on new challenges.

There is a direct line from the first humans to the Wright Brothers. Now that line has come to us today. It took millions and millions of years for the first humans to fly an airplane, but there were only 57 years between Orville Wright flying his

Wright Flyer 120 feet to Yuri Gagarin flying his *Vostok 1* into space on 12 April 1961. There were only 65 years stretching from a small jump at Kitty Hawk to the first voyage to the Moon in December 1968. Only six months after that, the first humans walked on the Moon. Since October 31, 2000, there have been at least three people in space at all times and sometimes many more than that.

We have come a long way, and we keep going. The stories in this book show how we have become space travelers. You will read about different ways we explore and live in space. On one hand, people have traveled to space, and they continue to live and work there. There are many plans for people to keep doing this. Eventually, we may leave Earth for other planets.

On the other hand, living and working in space presents many dangers. Space researchers like to say the universe is trying to kill you. This is just a saying, but it is true that humans evolved to live only on this planet. So, leaving Earth means creating the conditions to support life. Meeting those challenges gives us confidence to meet even more challenges ahead. This is one reason why we go to space.

Sending people to space is only one way to explore, however. Another way is to create machines to explore for us. In some ways, this makes studying space much easier. A machine does not need to breathe. It does not need food or water. It can survive in many difficult and dangerous environments. However, these machines cannot work on their own. People are needed to build them and make them work. The information they send back teaches us about other worlds, and even space itself.

There have been many more robotic space missions than human ones. Machines have been our eyes and ears, our tools to go to more and more distant places. We now have close-up pictures and other information from every planet that goes around the Sun.

Many countries are involved in sending people and machines

to other worlds. We work together because the Earth is our common home. By exploring space, we come together to create opportunities that we cannot create alone.

Space exploration is expensive. Space exploration is difficult. Space exploration is dangerous. So why do we do it? Humans have a passion to explore, to go somewhere new. When we do that, we experience the beauty and joy of a larger world. This teaches us about ourselves. When we explore space, we learn more about the Earth. We make our common culture richer, and we become something greater than we were before.

No one is alive who was born before the Wright brothers flew at Kitty Hawk. For everyone on Earth, airplanes have always been a fact of life. At some point, no one will be alive who was born before Yuri Gagarin flew in space. For people under 20, machines have been working on Mars every day of their lives. Living in space is now part of the human experience, and it gives meaning and inspiration to our life on Earth.

REFLECTION

1. Do you want to fly in space? What do you think it will be like?
2. It has been just over 100 years since the Wright Brothers flew the first airplane. What you think humans will do in the next 100 years?

THE FIRST STEPS IN SPACE

Space is both very close and very far away. The line between the air and space is only 80 kilometers from the ground (about 50 miles). A person could walk that far in two or three days. The Moon, however, is 384,400 kilometers (238,900 miles) away. That is like driving around Earth 10 times.

A famous American news reporter, Walter Cronkite, once said that the main achievement of the 20th Century was humans landing on the Moon. The nine Apollo trips to the Moon tell the story of that great achievement. Apollo 8 was the first time any human had gone to the Moon, while Apollo 11 was the first time a human walked on the Moon.

Humans have only gone as far as the Moon. However, we have sent space missions beyond the Moon. These missions have explored all the planets in the solar system. Each mission has sent back photographs and information. They teach us that the universe is a very strange and interesting place.

EARLY ACHIEVEMENTS

In the 1950s and 1960s, the United States and the Soviet Union raced each other to see who could control space. Each also wanted to do it first. This was known as the Space Race.

The first machine to circle the Earth was Sputnik 1. The small satellite was sent into space by the Soviet Union in 1957. A month later, the USSR sent the first live creature into space. The dog Laika traveled inside Sputnik 2, but she did not survive the trip.

The Soviet Union was also the first to send an object of any kind to the Moon. Luna 1 flew by on 4 January 1959. Luna 3 provided the first pictures of the far side of the Moon in October of that same year. The USSR was thus the first country to explore the Moon up close.

Perhaps the greatest achievement for the Soviet Union came in April of 1961. Cosmonaut Yuri Gagarin became the first human to experience space. He rode in his ship, the *Vostok 1*, one time around the Earth. Gagarin's flight was full of danger. The *Vostok 1* did not work as planned. Coming back down to Earth, the ship was traveling too fast. Gagarin survived forces 12 times greater than gravity and had to jump, using a parachute, from seven kilometers in the air. Unsurprisingly, the trip was Gagarin's only flight into space.

Gagarin said the flight gave him a new perspective about life on Earth. "When I orbited the Earth in a spaceship, I saw for the first time how beautiful our planet is. Mankind, let us preserve and increase this beauty, and not destroy it!"

LEAVING EARTH

The United States and the Soviet Union were the first countries to explore space. The United States created the National Aeronautics and Space Administration (NASA) in 1958 to carry out

American plans. NASA has been very successful. It was the first to send missions to every planet in the solar system. The United States was also the first country to visit a comet, a mixture of ice and dust that travels from very far away. The U.S. was also the first to visit an asteroid, which is like a very large rock, but it is smaller than a planet or most moons.

NASA's Mariner 2 was the first spacecraft to visit another planet, Venus. The small ship arrived in December of 1962. Mariner 2 discovered that Venus was covered in clouds. These clouds trapped the Sun's heat next to the surface. As a result, Venus' air is hot enough to melt lead (a metal).

Four years later, the Soviet Union's Venera 3 became the first human-made object to impact another planet's surface when it crash-landed on Venus in March of 1966. Later Venera machines sent back the first data and pictures from Venus's surface. They had only a small amount of time before Venus' pressure and temperature destroyed them.

NASA's Mariner 4 was the first machine to visit Mars in July of 1965. The Russian Mars 2 became the first human object on Mars in 1971, though it failed upon landing. The American Mariner 9 was able to orbit (go in a circle around) Mars when it arrived at Mars in 1971. NASA's Viking 1, meanwhile, was the first machine to land successfully on Mars in September of 1976.

This information about Venus and Mars helped scientists decide to focus on Mars. While Venus is too hot and dangerous, Mars has temperatures that are closer to Earth's. Mars has been explored more than anywhere else beyond Earth. Overall, there have been 44 missions sent to the Red Planet, and more are planned.

Meanwhile, Mariner 10 became the first space ship sent to Mercury, the planet closest to the Sun, in March of 1974. At that point, just 17 years after Sputnik, every planet in the inner solar system had been visited by ships from Earth. However, Mercury would not be visited again until 2008 when NASA returned with the MESSENGER robot explorer. MESSENGER discovered ice in the shadows on Mercury's craters and evidence of extinct volcanoes before it crashed into the planet in March 2015.

THE MOON

NASA is most famous for sending people to the Moon. Frank Borman, James Lovell, and William Anders were the first people to travel there, on *Apollo 8* in December of 1968. In doing so, they became the first humans to go somewhere beyond Earth. They went around the moon, but they did not land on the moon.

Apollo 11 is probably the most famous space trip in history. Neil Armstrong and Edwin "Buzz" Aldrin were the first humans to walk on another world. Their ship, named *Eagle*, landed on the Moon in the area known as the Sea of Tranquility in July of 1969. At the same time, Michael Collins went around the Moon in the command ship named *Columbia*.

All in all, 24 people made trips to the Moon, with three people going twice. The Cold War's "space race" may have started the missions, but science and exploration quickly became the goal. The Apollo program was about the human need to learn. When Armstrong took his first steps on the Moon, he spoke the famous words: "That's one small step for a man, one giant leap for mankind." The last man on the Moon, Gene Cernan, said much the same thing at the end of Apollo 17. Before lifting off, he said, "We leave as we came and, God willing, as we shall return: with peace and hope for all mankind."

GOING EVEN FURTHER

NASA is most famous for the Moon missions, but the trips to distant planets may be more important. Pioneer 10 was the first machine to visit Jupiter in December of 1973. This was the first trip to the outer planets.

Saturn had its first visitor in September of 1979 when the NASA robot Pioneer 11 flew by the planet with the famous rings. Saturn has been visited three more times since then. The last time was the Cassini-Huygens journey. The Cassini-Huygens project was a partnership between NASA and the European Space Agency. Cassini released the European Huygens robot, which was the first object to land anywhere further from the Sun than Mars. It set down on Saturn's moon Titan in January of 2005.

The successful visit to Titan led to other collaborations. NASA and the European Space Agency also visited a comet, Giacobini-Zinner. The International Cometary Explorer flew by in September of 1985.

The NASA space ships Voyager 1 and 2 opened up the outer solar system to humans in the 1970s and 1980s. Both ships flew by Jupiter and Saturn. Voyager 2 was also the first ship to visit the ice giants Uranus (in 1986) and Neptune (in 1989). This remains the only time either planet has been visited.

Voyager 1 became the first ship to leave our solar system. It passed beyond the Sun's wind in August 2012. It is expected to send back data about the gas and dust between the stars until the mid-2020s.

Gaspra was the first asteroid to host a human visit. The little rock is part of the asteroid belt, a group of smaller rocks that go around the Sun between Mars and Jupiter. The NASA space ship *Galileo* flew by in October of 1991. *Galileo* would go on to become the first spacecraft to stay at and explore Jupiter, which it did from 1995 to 2003.

Some planets are so small, they are called dwarf planets. The first two dwarf planets to receive a visit were Ceres and Pluto in 2015. NASA's *Dawn* spacecraft arrived at Ceres in March of that year after visiting the asteroid Vesta. It has made many discoveries, including volcanoes that shoot out ice!

NASA's *New Horizons* spacecraft arrived at Pluto in July of

2015. Pluto is so far away that it took the space ship nine years to get there. After leaving Earth, *New Horizons* was traveling so fast it went past the Moon in nine hours, a trip that took the Apollo astronauts three days!

Pluto is smaller than the Moon, but *New Horizons* found that the dwarf planet was very active. Ice mountains as tall as many mountains on Earth float on plains of liquid nitrogen, a very cold substance that is about as thick as toothpaste. Like Ceres, Pluto also has volcanoes that send out ice instead of lava.

Pluto is so far away that *New Horizons* had to explore without human control. Commands sent from Earth took four and a half hours to reach the small space ship. (*New Horizons* is about the size of a piano.) Also, any message sent by *New Horizons* took another four and a half hours to come back to Earth. Engineers had to design special computer programs so the computers could make decisions by themselves.

New Horizons is now heading for the most distant world ever explored. It is scheduled to fly by an object called "2014 MU69" in January of 2019. This distant asteroid is over 6.5 billion kilometers from Earth. Commands from Earth will take almost six hours to reach *New Horizons*!

The European Space Agency was the first to land on a comet. The *Rosetta* spaceship arrived at Comet 67P/Churyumov–Gerasimenko in 2014. It released a tiny machine named Philae, about the size of a coffee table, which landed on the surface to gather information. *Rosetta* also set down on the comet just before its power ran out in 2016.

More nations than ever before are going into space. India, for example, became the first Asian nation to explore Mars. Its Mangalyaan, or Mars Orbiter Mission, has been orbiting Mars since September 2014. The United Arab Emirates also plans to send a mission to Mars in the 2020s.

China has sent many people and robots into space. Yang Liwei became the first person from China to go into space in

October 2003. The Chinese have a small station in space now, and they plan to send a bigger one soon. China also plans send people to the Moon and Mars.

THE FUTURE

Space exploration is a job being taken up by many nations now. More and more countries are sending people and machines to space. This means that the technology will also get better and better.

Space exploration gives us all reasons to be proud. It makes our culture rich and helps us to solve problems. When we explore our solar system, we explore our home and learn about our possible future. As more time and resources are spent on building this technology, who knows what the next 60 years will bring?

REFLECTION

1. What is surprising about human missions into space?
2. Should countries work together to explore space?

FROM FAILURE TO SUCCESS

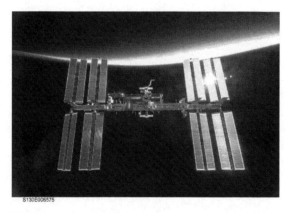

S130E006575

The International Space Station is the result of cooperation from 27 countries, and is the largest human-built thing ever to fly in space. (Photo credit: NASA/JSC)

Humans cannot survive in space, so sending a human outside our atmosphere is difficult. It takes many engineers and scientists a long time to develop the technology. Governments need to make careful decisions about their purpose. Who will control the projects, the military or a special government agency?

In the early days of space exploration, the Soviet Union and the United States struggled with these decisions in different ways. While both made mistakes, they each advanced the technological capabilities that made living in space a reality.

WHAT IS DYNA-SOAR/MOL?

The Soviet Union and the United States were in conflict from the end of World War II to the final days of the Soviet Union in the early 1990s. This was called the Cold War because the two countries did not fight with weapons, but they competed in other ways. One way was the race to explore space. During this Space Race that lasted from the 1950s to the 1970s both nations made historic achievements.

Both countries asked the question, "What part of a country's government will control a country's efforts in space?" The Soviet Union and, more recently China, chose to give control to their military. The United States chose a different path. The Americans put government workers in control of their space exploration. However, the American military was not happy with that plan.

THE SOVIET PLAN

In the 1950s the Soviet Union was a super power. Technological achievements like rockets showed their abilities. In 1957, the Soviets shocked the world by sending the world's first satellite,

Sputnik, into space. People around the world could see the tiny point of light travel over their heads. Some were amazed, while others were scared. If someone could put a satellite into space, could they send a bomb around the world too?

People could not answer that question because the Soviet military controlled the space program. It was done in secret and closed off from the public. The world only found out about their achievements after they happened. This made many people in the rest of the world worried. What else could the Russian military do? Were they a threat? Did they plan to use space to make war?

THE UNITED STATES' PLAN

In the 1950s, the U.S. was the other superpower in the world. Instead of giving control of space flight to the military, President Dwight Eisenhower made a different decision. He wanted public participation in science. He wanted scientists, businesspeople, and educators to be involved.

When Eisenhower created the National Aeronautics and Space Administration (NASA) in 1958, he took a risk. The world could watch American successes and failures on their newly invented televisions. Space would be explored for science, and not for war.

However, many Americans were also worried. If one country had a military advantage in space, it would be hard to challenge in a war. Because the Soviet Union's military controlled that country's space efforts, the American military felt they had to respond. They wanted to have a military role in space, even if NASA was in charge.

The Russians' military goals were not known, so the U.S. Air Force made many plans. One plan was to build bases on the Moon! However, most of their plans were closer to the Earth. The Air Force's leaders created two proposals to give the U.S. military a strong presence in space.

X-20/DYNA-SOAR

Just after Sputnik, the Air Force decided to build their own space ship. The plan was to create a winged ship like an airplane. They called the project the X-20, also named Dyna-Soar. At the time, the Air Force and NASA were working together on the highest and fastest airplane built at that time. It was called the X-15, and the Air Force hoped to use technology from the X-15 to design the X-20.

The plan for X-20 was simple. Dyna-Soar would lift off on top of a rocket. Then it would use its own engines to travel into space. The Dyna-Soar would fly around the world at high speed. Then it would come back to Earth and land like a glider at any Air Force base.

They expected Dyna-Soar to achieve many military goals. The Air Force planned to use it for spying and delivering weapons. They wanted to send people through space to anywhere in the world within hours.

However, the Dyna-Soar project had problems. The first problems were technical. When a spacecraft comes back to Earth, it is going very fast. Pushing against the air makes the outside get very, very hot. Engineers had to create a material that would not melt and was still light enough to go into space. This material did not exist yet, so engineers would have to build and test a heat-proof material. This research was very expensive, and the program's leaders had to fight for more money.

Also, developers wanted Dyna-Soar to glide to a landing after slowing down in space. No spacecraft had ever done that before. Engineers would have to figure out if that was possible. One small mistake could lead to the death of humans on board. This took time, which cost even more money.

Eventually, the government decided that the project cost too much. Also, with NASA sending people into space, the government did not need a "spaceplane." The X-20 Dyna-Soar project ended in December of 1963 before a working model was ever built. The failed project cost $410 million.

All was not lost however. Dyna-Soar's failure led to other achievements. The research was used on designs for many Air Force airplanes. In fact, plans for the Dyna-Soar helped later engineers design the Space Shuttle.

MANNED ORBITING LABORATORY

After Dyna-Soar, the Air Force had other plans. They tried to build the world's first space station, called the "Manned Orbiting Laboratory" or MOL. NASA at that time was sending two people at a time into space in the Gemini program. That program was part of the country's plans to learn how to fly to the Moon.

The Air Force had big plans for the MOL. It would use an empty rocket body as a home for two astronauts. They would fly there using a special Gemini space ship. The Air Force astronauts would connect to the MOL. Then they would travel through a special tunnel into the station where they would live and work.

The astronauts could stay in space for a month. In that time, they would use a large telescope to spy on the Soviet Union or other places, and do different military tasks. The MOL would not have weapons. Its job was to help the military from a safe location above Earth.

After finishing their jobs, the astronauts would return to Earth. Then another group of Air Force astronauts would be sent to the MOL on another job. The Air Force planned to use the MOL until well into the 1970s as a base for space operations.

The MOL faced many years of delays. Like with Dyna-Soar, the research and planning was expensive, and engineers needed to invent new technologies. Members of the government argued that space should be explored by NASA for science and not used by the Air Force. That argument won, and the MOL ended in 1969 after the Air Force had spent over $1 billion.

UNEXPECTED BENEFITS

Both the Soviet Union and United States decided that space ships were too expensive to achieve military goals. The Manned Orbiting Laboratory and Dyna-Soar were never built. However, the research was very important for the peaceful use of space. NASA sent up its first space station, Skylab, in 1973. Many of the designs for Skylab, including using an empty rocket as the station's main body, came directly from the Air Force's designs for the MOL.

We never know where scientific research will lead. While both projects did not deliver very many military benefits, research helped advance other peaceful projects. As many scientists will tell you, many of our best achievements began as failures.

REFLECTION

1. Should a country's space program be a scientific agency, or a military agency? Should a space program be public (run by the government) or private (run by private companies)?
2. Some people say that engineers and scientists are not creative. Does this story support or challenge that idea?

4

SPACE STATIONS BECOME A REALITY

Riding a space ship is a great way to get to and from space. However, once in space, astronauts need somewhere to live and work. In the 1960s and 1970s, travelers went to the Moon. Now, they travel to and from space stations.

The largest station going around Earth right now is the International Space Station. It is an example of international cooperation for a common goal. That goal is to expand humanity's knowledge by doing scientific research. Everything is different there because with almost no gravity, there is no sense of up and down. Plants grow in different ways. Water moves in different ways. Human bodies change in different ways. Scientists study all of this and more on the International Space Station

At least three people have always been in space since 2000. The ship itself is the largest single structure to orbit Earth. It is big enough to cover a football field, and it has science labs from the United States, Russia, Europe, and Japan. Over 20 countries have joined together to work on it. However, it is only one of many space stations.

EARLY IDEAS

Humans have long dreamed about creating a human settlement among the stars. The first description of a space station was in a short story called "The Brick Moon." It was written by an American named Edward Everett Hale in 1869, 100 years before humans walked on the Moon.

In 1952, German-born engineer Wernher von Braun came up with a plan for making a real space station. Von Braun proposed a very large wheel 76 meters wide that would spin to provide artificial gravity. His model became famous in many stories. A similar design appeared in the movie *2001: A Space Odyssey* and in the episode "A Wheel in Space" in the English television series *Doctor Who*. Though many people have written about it, no space station like this has ever been built.

SALYUT

The Soviet Union became the first country to build and fly space stations. Between 1971 and 1986, Russians flew on six Salyut space stations. The name means "salute" or "fireworks" in Russian. *Salyut 1* was the first of these stations. It was sent to space in April 1971. The first people to live on it were the *Soyuz 11* crew of Georgy Dobrovolsky, Vladislav Volkov, and Viktor Patsayev from June 7 to June 30 of that year. Sadly, there was an air leak on their space ship when they came back to Earth. By the time the ship landed, all three men were dead.

The tragedy of *Soyuz 11* did not stop the Salyut program. Russian engineers changed the *Soyuz* space ship to make it safer. The changes worked, and the Russians still use the Soyuz space ship today. In fact, Soyuz is the single most successful space ship in human history. In fact, China's *Shenzhou* ship is based on the Soyuz design.

Salyut 1 ran out of fuel and burned up coming back to Earth in October 1971. The Russians' next three attempts to send a station to space failed, but they kept trying. *Salyut 3* was a success and was in space in 1974 and 1975. Unlike *Salyut 1*, *Salyut 3* was a military space station. Cosmonauts Yuri Artyukhin and Pavel Popovich tested spy cameras and even a cannon during their stay. *Salyut 4* was a civilian station, and *Salyut 5* was the last military station.

The most successful Salyut stations were the last two, numbers 6 and 7. *Salyut 6* flew from September 1977 to July 1982. It showed that humans could live and work in space for long periods of time. *Salyut 6* was visited 16 times by an international crew. Vladimír Remek from Czechoslovakia became the first person to travel in space from a nation outside the United States or the Soviet Union; Arnaldo Tamayo Méndez from Cuba was the first black and the first Hispanic person in space; and Phạm Tuân from Vietnam became the first Asian person in space. *Salyut 7*, which followed, had many problems, but its research helped engineers when they developed the Mir space station.

SKYLAB

The first American space station was Skylab. The station lasted from 1973 to 1979 before it came back to Earth. It had a workshop for medical experiments. It also had the first tools in space especially meant to study the Sun. Flying above the air and clouds, Skylab astronauts could study the Sun with space telescopes. They did not have to wait for a clear day!

Skylab was built from an empty rocket. However, it had problems as soon as it was sent into space. As the rocket lifted off, a piece on the side came off. As it separated, it tore off the shield needed to protect the station from small meteors and the Sun's heat. It also destroyed one of the solar panels, needed to get energy from the Sun. The damage also kept the other solar panel from moving into place.

The first trip to the station was Skylab 2. It was led by Charles "Pete" Conrad Jr. along with Joseph Kerwin, a doctor, and Paul Weitz. Their first job was to fix the damaged station. They put up a new shield and managed to move the damaged solar panel into the right place. When that solar panel moved into place, it knocked Conrad and Kerwin off the station! They began to float away. Fortunately, they were tied to the station with ropes, and they made it back safely.

Two other groups of people would live and work on Skylab. All in all, nine people went there between 1973 and 1974. Their work taught us a lot about the Sun, as well as how people can live and work in space.

MIR

Mir was a Russian space station. The name Mir means "peace" in Russian. The name showed the station was for science and exploration. Mir lasted beyond the end of the Soviet Union, which broke apart into Russia and other states in 1991.

The station had seven main sections. These were all sent into space between 1986 and 1996. Once it was completed, Mir hosted many international visitors, including both Syrian and Afghan nationals. It was also visited by an American space shuttle eleven times as part of the Shuttle-Mir program. This cooperation between the Russian and American space programs was the beginning of other joint work in space.

Science was Mir's main reason for existence. Doctors learned a lot about the effects of long stays in space on the human body. One visitor, Valeri Polyakov, set the record for a single stay in space of 437 days! Also, the first crop of space wheat was grown on Mir. The wheat seeds grew and produced new seeds. This was an important event because it showed that humans can produce their own food in space.

But Mir also had problems. Two times, fires broke out on the space station. Once, a sudden power loss caused the station to tumble through space. Another time, a supply ship crashed into the station. This accident damaged a solar panel and part of the station. Air started leaking, and the astronauts were in danger. To close that section off, cosmonaut Sasha Lazutkin and British-American astronaut Michael Foale cut through cables with a kitchen knife! Their quick action saved the station.

When the Russians joined the effort to build the International Space Station, the Russian space agency Roskosmos decided that Mir had to end. It was too expensive to have both. One of the engineers who designed Mir, Vladimir Semyachkin, had this to say about the station.

"It's a shame," he said. "Our child, who we gave birth to so many years ago ... we're going to have to put it to sleep. But, on the other hand, we understand that sometimes there's nothing to be done.... One cannot sit, as it were, on two chairs at the same time. Nevertheless, despite this sorrow with ... regard to Mir, we none-theless do look forward to the future with a great deal of hope."

The last visitors left in April 2000. The station burned up coming back to Earth in March 2001.

THE INTERNATIONAL SPACE STATION

The Americans and Russians competed in the Space Race in the 1960s. However, after the Cold War ended, the two countries decided they could do more in space together than either country could alone. In September 1993, American Vice President Al Gore and Russian Prime Minister Viktor Chernomyrdin agreed on plans for a new space station, which eventually became the International Space Station. It would be the biggest space station ever built. It also became the biggest international engineering project. Today, twenty-seven countries are part of the project.

The space station has many parts, called modules. The first module was a Russian one called *Zarya*, which means "Dawn." It was sent to space in November 1998. By 2011, astronauts had put together over 159 parts in over 1,000 hours of space walking. Space walking is not easy. It is also very dangerous. Astronauts have to wear suits that have their own air systems, and helmets that limit what they can see. The men had to build the station while floating and wearing thick gloves. They were attached to the station with special ropes to keep them from floating off into space.

Sometimes space walks did not go as planned. In 2013, Italian astronaut Luca Parmitano noticed water leaking into his helmet while on a space walk. By the time he got back inside, his helmet was almost full of water. Parmitano had this to say about his experience: "The skills of our engineers and the technology surrounding us make things appear simple when they are not, and perhaps we forget this sometimes. Better not to forget."

Today, the International Space Station (ISS) is so big that people can see it from Earth. Sunlight reflects off its solar panels, making it very bright. Sometimes, if the angle is just right, it is brighter than anything except the Sun and the Moon.

The station is also the most expensive space project ever built. Its total cost will be $150 billion. It is expected to last until 2024, maybe longer. During that time, it will teach us many things about how to live in space. If people are ever going to go to Mars, they are going to have to be in space for many months, or even years.

The first group of people to live on board the station, known as Expedition 1, were American commander William Shepherd and Russians Yuri Gidzenko and Sergei Krikalev. They were sent into space 30 October 2000. There have been at least three people on board the ISS every single day since then.

Long stays in space can be hard for astronauts. Their bodies need gravity to work properly. Without gravity, muscles start to break down and bones break easily. People on board the station need to exercise at least two hours every day to stay strong. The equipment they use is designed to work without gravity.

Also, eating can be very different on board the station. Food can be heated in ovens, but not on stoves because it would just float away. Salt and pepper have to be mixed in liquids. An astronaut trying to sprinkle pepper on his soup would see it float away.

By solving large and small problems related to life in space, the International Space Station has shown us that when many countries work together, they can achieve great things. There has never been a project like the International Space Station. Some people think it is a model for a future Mars mission. It serves as a symbol of what countries can achieve in the future.

FUTURE STATIONS

There are many plans to replace the International Space Station. NASA hopes to build the Deep Space Gateway sometime in the 2020s. This will be a space station near the Moon. It will serve as a base for travelers going to Mars and other places.

China also has put small stations in space. The Tiangong-1 laboratory went up in 2011, and Tiangong-2 was sent to space in 2016. They are helping Chinese engineers design a much larger station. China plans to build a space station about half the size of Mir. They hope to send it into space in 2018 and 2019.

Also, many companies have plans to build private space stations. These include plans for everything from inflatable stations to wheels in space like von Braun's design.

The dream of living and working in space has been a challenge. However, that has not stopped humans from working for this goal. There are many inventions that keep us healthy, cure diseases and increase our quality of life that came from space technology. When humans achieve one thing, it gives us confidence to achieve much more.

Some day in the future, many humans may spend their whole lives off the Earth. The technology of that future day will come from the work being done today.

REFLECTION

1. Scientists are learning to grow food and how to protect the human body in space. How will this be useful in the future?
2. What would you see on a space walk? How would it make you feel?

III

HUMANS ON THE MOON

Apollo 11 landed on the Moon at the Sea of Tranquility on July 20, 1969. This photo is of Buzz Aldrin walking on the Moon. Neil Armstrong, who took the photograph, is reflected in Aldrin's helmet. (Credit: NASA)

In space, the Moon is right next door. If a country is going to explore space, it makes sense that one of the first targets would be our neighbor. However, going to the Moon was an expensive thing to do. What could convince a country to spend billions of dollars to go there?

Many people think the only reason the United States went to the Moon was to beat the Soviet Union. It became a Cold War contest. Others say that the Moon is an obvious place to go. Even without the Cold War, the Moon is a place for scientific study. Going there helped us learn more about our own planet. It also gave us technology that led to things like cell phones, personal computers and medical achievements. Going to the Moon gave us confidence to learn and innovate more than we ever dreamed. If we can put a person on the Moon, what else can we do?

5

TO THE MOON

In 1961, American President John F. Kennedy promised people that the United States would go to the Moon during the 1960s. Between 1968 and 1973, humans went to the Moon nine times. However, the work to explore the Moon went far beyond those nine voyages.

During that time, the National Aeronautics and Space Administration worked for that goal. Along the way there were many successes and failures. After a lot of work, though, the dream of landing humans on the Moon came true.

THE DECISION TO GO

On 5 March 1961, Alan Shepard became the first American in space. His "Freedom 7" flight lasted only 15 minutes. Just 20 days later, President John F. Kennedy said in a speech to Congress that he believed "this nation should commit itself, to send a man to the Moon by the end of this decade, and return him safely to the Earth."

There were two main reasons why Kennedy made the jump

from a 15-minute spaceflight to going to the Moon. The first reason was scientific. Kennedy and his advisors knew there was a lot to learn from visiting the Moon. No one knew how the Moon had formed or even how old it was. Also, building the machines to go there would involve technology that did not yet exist. Going to the Moon was a chance to leap forward in knowledge. It was an investment in the future.

In a speech at Rice University in Houston in September 1962, Kennedy laid out this vision when he said, "We choose to go to the Moon. We choose to go to the Moon in this decade and do the other things, not because they are easy, but because they are hard, because that goal will serve to organize and measure the best of our energies and skills, because that challenge is one that we are willing to accept, one we are unwilling to postpone, and one which we intend to win."

The second reason had more to do with politics than science. The United States was behind in the "Space Race." The Soviet Union had sent the first human object into space, Sputnik, in 1957. They followed this by sending the first human into space, Yuri Gagarin, in early 1961.

These were great political victories for the Russians, but Kennedy was determined to win. In that same speech at Rice, he said, "The exploration of space will go ahead, whether we join in it or not, and it is one of the great adventures of all time, and no nation which expects to be the leader of other nations can expect to stay behind in the race for space."

By setting the Moon as a goal, Kennedy was able to create a new contest. He took a risk that this time the United States would get there first.

HOW TO GET THERE

NASA had been ordered to go to the Moon. Now, they had to

learn how to do it. Engineers and scientists gathered to solve the problems and come up with a plan.

The first idea was a direct method. In this plan, NASA would build a giant rocket called Nova. Nova would carry a ship that contained up to three people. The ship would travel straight to the Moon and land. Then it had to lift off and return to Earth. The problem with this plan was that the Moon ship would be extremely heavy. A very big and complicated rocket would have to be built. That would cost more money than NASA could spend.

Another idea was to send many small pieces of the Moon ship into space around Earth. Astronauts would build the ship there and then fire the engines to go to the Moon. This plan was very difficult, and would involve many different trips to space. If any one of them failed, it would cause a delay.

Eventually an engineer working at the Langley Research Center in Maryland, John C. Houbolt, got involved. Houbolt did not like either plan, so he drew up a different one that he called Lunar Orbit Rendezvous.

Houbolt wanted to use the large Saturn V rocket to lift two space ships into space at the same time. One ship, the command module, would carry three people to the Moon. The other ship, the lunar module, would be connected to the first. When the ships got close to the Moon, two astronauts would get into the lunar module. They would ride down to the Moon and land. Then they would fly back to the remaining astronaut, who was still in the command module. After reconnecting the lunar module to the command module, the three would return to Earth in the command module.

Houbolt was brave to suggest this idea. Most engineers at NASA were trying to decide between the expensive and heavy Nova plan and the difficult Earth orbit plan. Houbolt wrote a letter directly to his boss Robert Seamans in November 1961. In the letter, he described his idea for Lunar Orbit Rendezvous and said that his plan was the only one that would allow NASA to land people on the Moon before 1970.

NASA chose Houbolt's idea for two reasons. One, they could build Saturn rockets with existing factories. The other was that the Nova plan might not be possible before the end of the 1960s. Houbolt's idea won over most other engineers at NASA, including the lead rocket engineer Wernher von Braun. Houbolt went down in history as the man who helped humans land on the Moon *and* return to Earth.

GEMINI

Between them, the United States and Soviet Union sent 26 different machines to the Moon before the first human visit. The Russians were also trying to get a person to the Moon. However, they kept having problems. The rocket they wanted to use, the N1, was the largest rocket ever built. However, it exploded during tests, and it never flew successfully.

The Soviets built a space ship, the Zond, to send people to the Moon. Zond 5, with only turtles, worms, and insects on board, went around the Moon in September 1968, but it did not return to the right place on Earth. In November of 1968, Zond 6 went around the Moon without passengers, but its parachute failed and it crashed. These failures meant the Soviet Union did not send a human to the Moon.

The United States, meanwhile, stayed focused on Kennedy's goal. Project Gemini was NASA's second human space flight program. In 1965 and 1966, 10 Gemini flights went into space with two people on board. The flights helped them learn to do the necessary tasks for a moon landing. Among the things NASA did for the first time in Gemini were:

1. Leave the ship to work outside in a space suit.

2. Give astronauts experience living and working in space.
3. Stay in space for longer than a week.
4. Fly two ships together in space.
5. Dock (connect) one ship to another ship.

The final flight of the program was *Gemini XII* in November 1966. After that, NASA felt ready. The agency then turned its full attention to the Apollo program.

TRAGEDY AND SUCCESS

Unfortunately for NASA, there were many dark days before the Apollo program succeeded. Two months after *Gemini XII*, astronauts Virgil "Gus" Grissom, Edward White and Roger Chaffee were testing their space ship, *Apollo 1*, in Florida. During that test in January 1967, a spark set the oxygen in their ship on fire. Everything burned. The men could not open the door in time to escape, and all of them died within seconds.

Kennedy's goal of a moon landing before the end of the 1960s suddenly looked impossible. It took more than a year for NASA to learn what caused the *Apollo 1* fire, and how to fix it. Then it took even longer for a new ship to be designed and built.

While the Apollo space ships were being made, engineers were also building the Saturn V rocket. It was 110 meters high and the largest rocket ever to lift people into space. The rocket was the size of a 36-story building and weighed over three million kilograms. It had three major stages, which would fire one after the other. By the time all the stages fired, the Apollo space ship would be traveling over 40,000 kilometers per hour on its way to the Moon.

The Saturn V was tested twice before people were allowed on board. The first time, in a mission called Apollo 4, it worked perfectly. The second time, with the mission of Apollo 6, the rocket shook so much that part of it broke, and it flew off course. Von Braun and his engineers found and fixed the shaking problem quickly. By the end of 1968, the Saturn V was ready to carry people to the Moon.

In October 1968, *Apollo 7* was sent to circle Earth on a test flight with three people on board. *Apollo 7* tested the command and service module only, and did not have a lunar module along. The trip took over 10 days, and at the end, the moon ship was called a success.

Two months later, Frank Borman, James Lovell, and William Anders became the first human beings to see the Moon up close. *Apollo 8* was the first space mission to leave the Earth, circle around another world and return home. Borman, Lovell, and Anders became the first human beings to escape Earth's gravity and see both the far side of the Moon and then the entire Earth all at the same time.

One very important part of the plan could only be tested in space. The lunar module needed to land on the Moon and return. In March 1969, *Apollo 9* tested the lunar module in space around the Earth. Then, in May 1969, *Apollo 10* became the second human trip to the Moon. Astronauts Thomas Stafford and Eugene Cernan flew the lunar module *Snoopy* to within 15 kilometers of the Moon.

After *Apollo 10*, all of the main parts of the Apollo space ships had been tested in space. The only thing still to do was land on the Moon.

ONE SMALL STEP

In July 1969, the United States sent *Apollo 11* to the Moon. On board were commander Neil Armstrong, lunar module pilot Edwin "Buzz" Aldrin, and command module pilot Michael

Collins. *Apollo 11* was launched on July 16. Four days later, Armstrong and Aldrin successfully flew the lunar module named Eagle away from Michael Collins in the command module Columbia. Then the problems started.

Almost as soon as Eagle flew away from Columbia, Armstrong and Aldrin ran into trouble. The first problem was that the antenna kept losing connection with Mission Control in Houston, Texas. If this could not be fixed, the rules said that the mission would have to end. Luckily, the radio link was repaired quickly.

Just as that problem got fixed, alarms went off in Eagle. The computer on board was trying to do too many things. If this continued, the computer might shut down. Engineers back on Earth quickly discovered how to fix the problem by slowing down the computer's instructions. They told Armstrong and Aldrin to continue as planned.

The last problem almost ended the mission. Flying Eagle to about 30 meters over the Moon, Armstrong looked out the window. He did not see what he expected. Their planned landing site in the Sea of Tranquility was in the middle of a field of large rocks. Eagle could not land there. With very little fuel, Armstrong had to find another landing site.

A fuel alarm suddenly went off in *Eagle*. It told Armstrong and Aldrin that they had 30 seconds of fuel left before the engine would shut off. Just then, Armstrong saw a clear path. With 10 seconds of fuel left, Armstrong set down the ship. He then called out the famous words: "Houston, Tranquility Base here. The *Eagle* has landed." The time was exactly 8:18 p.m. GMT on 20 July 20 1969.

The original plan called for the two men to sleep in the ship before going outside. However, the two astronauts were too excited to sleep. Mission control gave them permission to continue, and after two hours of preparation, Armstrong became the first human being to set foot on the Moon. On the way to the Moon, Armstrong felt he was not just one person, but representing all the people of Earth. At that moment, he knew what to say. As he stepped out of *Eagle* and onto the Moon's dusty surface, he said, "That's one small step for a man, one giant leap for mankind."

Armstrong and Aldrin spent 18 hours on the Moon. They collected rock and dust samples, and put out scientific instruments. Three new minerals were discovered in the rock samples. One of them, armalcolite, was named after Armstrong, Aldrin, and Collins.

SIX MORE TIMES

The United States had achieved Kennedy's goal. However, *Apollo 11* was not the last flight to the Moon. NASA would return six more times. *Apollo 12* landed in the Ocean of Storms in November 1969. *Apollo 13* suffered an explosion on the way to the Moon. It went around and came back safely after a scary six days. *Apollo 14*, commanded by Alan Shepard, landed at the Fra Mauro region of the Moon in January 1971.

Apollo 15, 16, and *17* carried a small car with them. The lunar rover allowed astronauts to explore even more of the Moon. *Apollo 15* found a 4-billion-year-old piece of the Moon near Mount Hadley. This rock, called the "Genesis Rock," helped prove that the Moon had once been part of the Earth. The last trip, *Apollo 17*, spent three days at the Taurus-Littrow Valley. It was also the only mission to bring along a geologist, Harrison Schmitt.

Apollo 17 was commanded by Eugene Cernan, who was the last man on the Moon. As he got back into the lunar module *Challenger*, Cernan spoke to people watching on Earth:

I'm on the surface; and, as I take man's last step from the surface, back home for some time to come – but we believe not too long into the future – I'd like to just [say] what I believe history will record. That America's challenge of today has forged man's destiny of tomorrow. And, as we leave the Moon at Taurus-Littrow, we leave as we came and, God willing, as we shall return, with peace and hope for all mankind.

CONCLUSION

In the end, the Apollo program cost $25.4 billion. Spending that money realized a dream that stretched back to the first time anyone looked up and saw the Moon in the sky. In his speech at Rice University, President Kennedy had predicted the benefits of going to the Moon when he said: "The growth of our science and education will be enriched by new knowledge of our universe and environment, by new techniques of learning and mapping and observation, by new tools and computers for industry, medicine, the home as well as the school." All of this came true.

Right now, NASA has no plans to return to the Moon. However, that does not mean the agency has stopped studying the Moon. Among other machines, the Lunar Reconnaissance Orbiter studies the Moon from the sky. The LRO has also sent back pictures of the Apollo landing sites, showing the tools and machines the astronauts left behind.

Other countries have announced plans for Moon missions. China has even said it plans to build a moon base. Other people hope to use the Moon to send trips to Mars. It is clear that Apollo was only the beginning.

REFLECTION

1. Apollo astronauts felt that they represented everyone on Earth when they went to the Moon. Do you agree?
2. What does the moon landing teach you about humans?

6

APOLLO 13: A DIFFERENT KIND OF SUCCESS

OVERVIEW

Between 1968 and 1972, the United States sent nine missions to the Moon. Eight of those missions achieved their goals. One, *Apollo 13*, faced disaster. Instead of a mission of science and exploration, *Apollo 13* became an example of courage in the face of failure.

The lives of all three men on board *Apollo 13* depended on a few engineers. With very little technology, those engineers faced problems they had never seen before. Their equipment was less powerful than the mobile phones we use today. There were many times when the engineers feared the astronauts might die in space, but they did not give up.

THE ASTRONAUTS

James Lovell was the commander of *Apollo 13*. This was his fourth flight into space. He was most famous for being one of the first men to fly to the moon on *Apollo 8*. Because *Apollo 8* did not land on the Moon, Lovell was looking forward to his first moon walk on this mission.

The other two astronauts had never been to space before. Fred Haise was the pilot of the lunar lander (the part of the ship that was supposed to land on the Moon). This was Fred Haise's only spaceflight.

Jack Swigert piloted the command module. He was supposed to fly around the Moon while Lovell and Haise landed. However, Swigert was a last-minute change. He wasn't supposed to be on *Apollo 13*. The original pilot, Thomas Mattingly, was exposed to measles the week before *Apollo 13* was going to lift off. Doctors were afraid Mattingly might get sick, and they told him he could not go. Swigert was chosen to go in his place four days before they left. Like Haise, this would be his only spaceflight.

THE SPACE SHIP

There were three parts to an Apollo spacecraft. The command module held the astronauts when flying to the Moon. They also got back into the command module when they returned to Earth. On *Apollo 13*, this part was named *Odyssey*.

The service module was connected to the command module. It held the machines that made the command module work. It also had rockets that would be used to push the spaceship to the Moon, and send it home to Earth. This was the part that would have problems on *Apollo 13*.

The lunar module was important because it would land on the Moon. It even had a name: Aquarius. After getting to the Moon, Lovell and Haise were to separate *Aquarius* from the command module and fly it down to the landing site. This small ship had two parts, an engine that would allow the astronauts to fly down to the Moon and space for the astronauts above. It also had an engine that would carry the astronauts back into space.

Aquarius was seven meters tall, and could break easily. It was so fragile that on Earth, it could barely support its own weight! It could only be flown in space. The ship was covered in thin insulation that was about as thick as three layers of aluminum foil. This layer also served as the ship's walls. A person could put their hand or foot straight through it, so everyone had to be very careful!

Apollo 13 lifted off from Florida on 11 April 1970. On the way to space, one of the five engines on the Saturn V rocket failed. It was not enough to stop them from reaching space. The failure might have caused the rocket to explode, and to this day, no one is sure why it didn't. It looked like *Apollo 13* was going to be a lucky flight.

"HOUSTON, WE'VE HAD A PROBLEM."

Everything was going according to plan. After 55 hours, controllers asked Jack Swigert to mix the oxygen in a tank on board *Odyssey*. In the cold of space, that oxygen gas was mostly frozen. A special machine heated and moved the oxygen to keep it from freezing solid. No one knew that this machine had an electrical problem. When Swigert turned it on, it made a spark. This spark caused the oxygen inside the tank to explode.

When the tank exploded, it damaged the other machinery around it. The explosion was so violent it ripped off the outer part of the service module.

After the explosion, Swigert called down to Mission Control with the famous words, "OK, Houston, we've had a problem here." Lovell then got on the radio to tell the controllers that *Odyssey*'s power was dropping and that gas was leaking into space. Without oxygen, the astronauts would not be able to breathe. Suddenly, the mood in the ship became very serious.

AROUND THE MOON

It was clear now that *Apollo 13* would not land on the Moon. Instead, the mission now had only one goal: bring Lovell, Swigert, and Haise back to Earth. "My thoughts went from the landing to wondering how we're all going to get home again," Lovell said.

The astronauts were in great danger. They would have to move into the lunar module Aquarius until just before coming back into the Earth's atmosphere. Only *Odyssey* could get them safely back to Earth.

They had two choices. They could turn around and come straight back, or they could go around the Moon first. Coming straight back would be faster, but they would have to use the big engine on the service module. The problem was that they did not know if it had been damaged in the explosion, so they chose to go around the Moon first. This was safer, but it would take longer.

The team quickly formed a plan. They decided to swing around the Moon. The astronauts used the tiny engine on *Aquarius* to get them onto the right path. Then they shut everything down to save power. It was going to be a very cold and dark journey.

THE LONG WAY HOME

On the way back to Earth, the problems just kept coming. When people breathe, we take in air and send out a gas called carbon dioxide. On board a space ship, a machine takes that carbon dioxide and filters it out of the air. The machine on board *Aquarius* was built to clean the air of two people breathing for two days. Now, it had to clean the air of three people for four days. The filters needed to be changed to keep the machine working, or the astronauts would run out of oxygen and die.

The filters were dangerously full of carbon dioxide. The astronauts could not use the filters in *Odyssey* because the parts there did not fit in *Aquarius*. In Houston, engineers struggled to solve the problem. They figured out a way to build a new filter with only the things that were already on the space ship. They instructed the astronauts to use pieces of *Odyssey*'s air machine, space suits, books, tape, and other things to make new filters. The astronauts then put the new filter into place and waited. Slowly the air began to clear. The filters worked! The men could stay alive to solve the next problem.

They also had to use the equipment in ways that had not been tested. They had to turn the *Odyssey*'s power off for days, and then they had to turn it back on again with the space ship in flight. No one had ever practiced that before. There was no guarantee that *Odyssey*'s power would come back on in the freezing cold of space.

One of the biggest mysteries was *Aquarius*. The tiny ship was made to travel from the command module to and from the Moon. Now they were using it to steer the larger ship back to Earth. To make matters worse, the tools needed to steer had been shut down to save power. The astronauts had only their eyes and brains to make difficult moves.

Then mission control realized that *Apollo 13* had drifted off course on the way back to Earth. This was very bad because if the ship did not hit Earth's atmosphere just right, it would either burn up or skip off into space. There would be no way to rescue the astronauts. Engineers on Earth worked with the astronauts in space to make an emergency plan. They fired up *Aquarius*'s engine and guided the ship by hand. The astronauts got back on target.

Astronauts, controllers, and engineers worked without a break for three days. Lovell said it was their focus that got them through each problem. "In a situation like that, there's only one thing to do. You just keep going," he said. He also added, "It's amazing the way people can respond so fast to get the job done."

NEARING HOME

Aquarius could not come back to Earth because it was not protected with a heat shield. When the crew separated the service module from *Odyssey*, the astronauts could see where the explosion had occurred. Lovell called it "a real mess."

Swigert then turned the power back on in *Odyssey* so the astronauts could move back there from *Aquarius*. Lovell and Haise stayed in *Aquarius* until *Odyssey* was ready just in case the command module did not turn back on. Lovell watched as the Earth got closer and closer in the window. Worried, he ordered Swigert to work faster. Controllers on the ground gave instructions, and Swigert did the work in time.

All three astronauts then moved into *Odyssey* and let go of the lunar module. "Farewell, Aquarius, and we thank you," called out Haise.

The astronauts had one more challenge. *Odyssey* had to reenter the Earth's atmosphere. This creates a lot of heat, which cuts off radio contact. Controllers had to wait for six long minutes before the tiny capsule dropped through the clouds. Finally, a voice came across the speakers. It was the astronauts, and they were alive. The craft splashed down in the Pacific Ocean on April 17, six days after lifting off.

A SUCCESSFUL FAILURE

Many people would call *Apollo 13* a failure. The people involved did not agree. After the flight, President Richard Nixon declared *Apollo 13* a successful mission. Flight director Gene Kranz called the mission "a successful failure." Lovell said much the same thing. "I would have liked to have landed on the Moon, but what we got out of this flight was also well worth it," he said.

What did they mean by that? *Apollo 13* was a chance for the astronauts, scientists, and engineers to create solutions to problems in space. Everyone had to work together to prevent disaster. They had to solve problems they could not have predicted. Scientists, engineers, and astronauts had to invent new ways to fly the spacecraft, and all in very little time.

In the end, *Apollo 13* was both unlucky and lucky, but it provided inspiration and confidence to continue exploring the Moon.

REFLECTION

1. Imagine you are an astronaut on the Apollo 13 mission. How do you feel? What do you do to stay calm?
2. Apollo 13 was called a "successful failure." What does this mean? Have you ever had a "successful failure"?

IV

THE PLANET NEXT DOOR

The tiny Sojourner can be seen studying a large rock after leaving the
Pathfinder lander in 1997. (Photo credit: ASA/JPL

The Earth is the only planet that we know has life. But is there
life anywhere else? Some say that finding life on any other planet
would prove that it exists all through the universe. It would help

answer two major questions: Who are we? Are we alone in the universe?

Near Earth, there are only a few places life could exist. One of them is Mars. The Red Planet is a cold, dry desert today. Its thin air is poison to people. However, it may have had an atmosphere and surface water at some time in the past. For this reason, humans have sent many machines to Mars, but ships with people on board are still many years away. What do you think would change if we learn that Mars supported life in the past? What about if it had life now? Would it change how you understand your place in the universe?

7

MARS THROUGH VIKING

OVERVIEW

Humans have been in Mars for a long time. They see its red color and bright light and become curious. When it is brightest, only four things are brighter: the Sun, Moon, Venus, and Jupiter. The Greeks and Romans named the planet Mars after their god of war because of its bloody red color.

The Greeks and Romans weren't the only cultures to name Mars for its color. In India, Mars was known as "Mangala," a Hindu god of war. The Babylonians called it "Nergal," after their god of fire and war. In China, its name is "Huo Hsing," and in Japan "Kasei." Both translate to "Fire Star." The Egyptians named it "Her Desher," which means "the red one." When Asaph Hall discovered Mars' two moons in 1877, he continued this theme. Hall named them Phobos and Deimos. In Roman stories, these were the god Mars' two horses, "Fear" and "Panic."

Today, Mars is the subject of much study. Learning more about Mars teaches us about planets and gives us a new way to look at the Earth. Mars is one-third the size of Earth, and the planets get close to each other every two years. While people have been to the Moon and not Mars, it is the Red Planet that has had more missions. Some scientists even joke that Mars has become the "Planet of Robots."

DREAMS AND REALITY

Galileo was the first person to see Mars through a telescope in 1608. Since then, many other scientists have looked at Mars in a telescope as well. On Earth our air moves because of heat, cold, and wind. This makes the things in telescopes look fuzzy and shimmer. Mars is close enough to see its surface through telescopes, but not very well. People also saw the surface change at different times of the year. This made Mars a puzzle. What caused these changes? Was it plants and life? Nobody knew.

It was big news when an American, Asaph Hall, discovered Mars's moons in 1877. Soon more scientists started to study Mars. The two most famous studies of Mars were done by an Italian, Giovanni Schiaparelli, and American, Percival Lowell. In 1888, Schiaparelli said he had discovered narrow lines on Mars. He called them "canali," an Italian word that means "channels," like a river valley. His drawings of Mars showed winding lines that looked natural. Unfortunately, the word was reported in English as "canals." Canals are rivers made by humans. Did it mean that someone had created Schiaparelli's "canali"?

Lowell built a large telescope in Arizona just to look at Mars. From there he said he saw more than natural channels. He said he saw canals and claimed these were signs of life. Lowell said he saw many narrow, straight lines on Mars. He said these canals were built to carry water from the polar ice caps to drier regions. Many of the maps Lowell drew were still in use when the first space ships arrived in the 1960s. However, the pictures showed a very different Mars.

Schiaparelli and Lowell were both talented astronomers, but their tools could not see as clearly as telescopes of today. Schiaparelli described many features that could have been just fuzzy views of real things, like highlands and dark areas. However, almost no one else saw the "canals" that Lowell described. As the scientist Carl Sagan once noted, in the end, Lowell may have let his imagination get in the way.

Many writers used these theories as the basis for stories about Mars. In *The War of the Worlds*, the Englishman H.G. Wells wrote about a race that invaded Earth because Mars had gotten too dry. The American writer Edgar Rice Burroughs wrote books about a man named John Carter who travels to Mars. Burroughs' books described a desert planet that residents called "Barsoom." Carter found beautiful Martian princesses and magnificent cities built along the canals.

It took the invention of space ships to find out what Mars was really like. When spacecraft eventually got to Mars, they sent back photos of craters, mountains, and deserts. What they did not show was water, canals, or signs of Martians. In fact, Mars looked more like the Moon than Barsoom.

FIRST VISITS

Sending space ships to Mars is really hard. As of 2017, 55 ships have lifted off to visit the Red Planet. Of those, only 27 have been successful. However, since 2000, there have been 16 Mars space ships and only four failures. This means humans are improving the technology for a journey of about 35 million miles.

The first ship to go to Mars and stay was Mariner 9. It arrived in November of 1971 and became the first space ship to go around another planet. Within a month, Mariner 9 was joined by Mars 2 and Mars 3, which were sent by the Soviet Union. Unfortunately, when all three ships arrived, Mars was completely covered by a dust storm!

Both Mars 2 and Mars 3 carried landers. The Mars 2 lander

failed. The Mars 3 lander became the first object to set down on Mars, but it failed 15 seconds after landing.

Mariner 9 was a total success. The Mars 2 and Mars 3 instruments were completely programmed before they left Earth. The dust storm meant that Mars was not going to cooperate with these plans. However, Mariner 9 had a different computer. Engineers could program it during the flight. This was useful because the dust storm did not clear until January of 1972.

By the time Mars came into view, Mars 2 and Mars 3 had shut off. They eventually returned 60 pictures between them. Almost all of them showed a fuzzy planet covered in dust. However, because engineers could change Mariner 9's plans, it sent back over 7,000 pictures of Mars.

Mariner 9 allowed humans to see ancient river beds, craters, and very large extinct volcanoes. One of these is the largest mountain in the solar system, named Olympus Mons. Olympus Mons is almost two-and-a-half times as high as Mt. Everest, the highest mountain on Earth. Mariner 9 pictures also showed the largest canyon system in the solar system. It was named the Mariner Valley, or *Valles Marineris*, after the space ship. The valley is 4,020 km (2,500 miles) long and would stretch across the entire North American continent if it were on Earth!

Mariner 9 ran out of fuel in October 1972 and was turned off. It is still going around Mars, but scientists expect it to burn up or crash by 2022.

VIKING

The Viking program was the next major study of Mars. It was made of four ships. They were sent into space by the United States in 1975 and arrived at Mars in the summer of 1976. Viking 1 arrived at Mars on 19 June 1976, and its lander set down in *Chryse Planitia* (the "Plain of Gold") on 20 July. This was seven years to the day after *Apollo 11* landed on the Moon. Viking

2 got there on 7 August 1976. Its lander set down on *Utopia Planitia* (the "Plain of Paradise") on 3 September 1976.

The Viking landers were each the size and weight of a small pickup truck. NASA had to use a combination of heat shields, parachutes, and rockets to get them to the ground safely. They helped us see Mars from the ground for the first time. The landers sent back pictures of sunsets, the Earth hanging in the sky, and rocks and deserts. The Viking orbiters up in space sent back information about Mars' air. They also made maps of the surface in detail.

Both landers were like chemistry laboratories on the Martian surface. They could pick up rocks and dirt and do experiments. They even looked for signs of life. So far, they have not found any.

The Viking program showed that Mars was a cold, dry place. Mars has less than one-tenth the air pressure of Earth. Its air is mainly made of carbon dioxide. Also, there's so little air on Mars that water cannot be liquid on the surface. Viking also found many dry river valleys and lake beds. The pictures proved that Mars once had surface water. That means that the air used to be thicker, and the temperature was warmer. But Viking could not answer this question: Where did all the water, heat, and air go? That would have to wait for later ships.

The Viking space ships and landers lasted much longer than expected. The Viking 2 orbiter was the first to shut down after a fuel leak in 1978. Next came the Viking 2 lander. Its power ran out in April 1980. The Viking 1 space ship ran out of fuel in August 1980.

Losing the Viking 1 lander was a sad story. In November 1982, an engineer sent instructions to improve the battery's use of power. However, the instructions accidentally caused the antenna to point in the wrong direction. Contact was lost forever, and the Viking program came to an end.

Viking was the end of the first wave of the exploration of

Mars. There would not be another successful trip to the Red Planet until 1996. Since then, however, Mars has been studied in great detail.

REFLECTION

1. In your opinion, how did people feel when they thought there was life on Mars?
2. How is the scientific truth about Mars exciting and/or disappointing?

8

HOW FAR AWAY IS MARS?

MARS AFTER VIKING

Every two years, Mars and Earth come close to each other. This is the best time to send ships. Of course, saying Mars and Earth are close may mean a different understanding of that word.

The distance between Earth and Mars always changes. Both go around the sun, but they travel at different speeds. Since Earth is closer to the Sun, it travels faster. Mars is farther from the Sun, so it goes slower. These differences mean it takes a lot of math to time a visit when the two planets are near each other.

When Mars is on the opposite side of the Sun from Earth, the two planets are as far apart as can be, and it is not a good time to send ships. The two planets at their farthest can be as much as 401 million km or 250 million miles apart. Every 26 months or so, we are on the same side of the Sun. When the two planets are lined up like this, with the sun on one side of the Earth and Mars on the opposite side, scientists call it *opposition*. This is when the planets are closest. The distance then is only about 55 million kilometers or 34 million miles.

The first two people to figure out these changing distances

were the Italian scientist and engineer Giovanni Cassini and the French astronomer Jean Richer in 1672. Cassini carefully measured how Mars looked against the stars in the background from Paris. At the same time, Richer did the same thing in Cayenne, French Guiana. Because of the distance between Cassini and Richer, Mars was in a different place against the distant stars in the background. This allowed the two scientists to measure the distance using simple math with a method known as "parallax."

Today, scientists measure the distance to Mars by counting how long it takes radio commands to get to our space probes and come back. The signals travel at the speed of light. By measuring how long it takes the commands to get to Mars and back, we can figure out how far the commands traveled.

Scientists sending ships to Mars have to know all of this. It takes anywhere from six to nine months to get a ship from Earth to Mars when the planets are closest. To time the launch date, planners have to count back that amount of time from opposition. Scientists call this a "launch window." Humans have taken advantage of nearly every launch window since 1996.

FAILURE AND SUCCESS

After Viking, only two of the next 10 attempts to get to Mars succeeded. There were many reasons for the losses. Most, including Japan's Nozomi, had parts fail while on the 11-month trip.

Another ship, the American Mars Climate Orbiter, failed for a different reason. When designing the computer program, engineers used metric units for how hard the engines should fire. However, the engine designers used Imperial units. No one discovered the mistake until the ship reached Mars only to burn up in the thin atmosphere.

Engineers try to learn from their mistakes as well as their

successes. Two attempts that did succeed were Mars Global Surveyor and the Pathfinder lander/Sojourner rover. Mars Global Surveyor arrived in September 1997. It was the first successful Mars trip since Viking.

Engineers flying Mars Global Surveyor used a new way to stay at Mars; it was called "aerobraking." When it got to the Red Planet, the ship flew in close. This allowed its long solar panels to act like wings. As the ship brushed against the thin air, it slowed down. This made it get to the right speed to stay around the planet, and neither crash nor fly by.

MGS stayed around Mars for nine years. It helped us learn about Martian weather, and it found signs of water near the surface. Pictures from its camera also helped find more places to land other ships.

Pathfinder also used a new method for landing on Mars. When it got there in July 1997, it slowed down behind a heat shield. Next, a parachute slowed it down even more, and then things got really interesting. Pathfinder was surrounded by air bags. With 350 meters to go, these filled with air. The ship was then lowered by a rope from its shell. Motors in the shell fired to slow things down even more. With 12 meters to go, Pathfinder dropped, bounced and rolled to a landing. Even better, this was all done at night!

Pathfinder had an interesting robot on board. It was a tiny vehicle named for the 19th Century African-American anti-slavery and women's rights fighter Sojourner Truth. Sojourner was the first rover (a vehicle with wheels) on Mars. It was very small, only 65 cm long. It was about the size of a large pillow. However, it allowed scientists to study places and rocks around Pathfinder.

TIME ON MARS

Since 2000, there have been many more successes than failures on Mars. Every single day there are engineers remotely working for, on, and around Mars. Also, there are many scientists working with the information those machines send back. Every day, we learn more. However, that research has led to some interesting problems.

Telling time on Mars is difficult. Scientists use machines on Mars to be our eyes and ears in exploring the planet. But humans working on Earth have days that are 24 hours long and years that are 365 days. On Mars, a day is 24 hours and 40 minutes. Scientists call it a "sol." A Martian year is 687 Earth days, or 669 sols.

Scientists have to decide what unit of time they're going to use. Many scientists just change their own clocks to tell time in sols. Some even wear two watches on their arms, one on Earth time and the other on Mars time! This allows them to be on the same daily pace as their robots.

How scientists solve this problem is important. If humans ever live on Mars, they are going to have to change from Earth days to sols. Their support staff on Earth are going to have to work that way as well.

WATER ON MARS

Mars has almost no water on the ground. The dirt and dust has less water than the Atacama Desert in Chile, the driest place on Earth. If people are ever going to live on Mars, they cannot bring all the food and water they need. They are going to have to find water to drink, and they need to grow food. The good news is that Mars has water. But where is it?

It has taken many ships from several countries to answer that question. There is so little air on Mars that water cannot stay liquid. It goes from ice to gas right away. To find water, we have to look on or under the ground.

Pictures taken by Europe's Mars Express, the American Mars Global Surveyor, and Mars Odyssey were the first to show water. Dark lines on the sides of craters and other slopes show up each Martian summer. They are caused by water seeping through the dust and dirt as it heats.

In 2003, the Spirit and Opportunity rovers also found evidence of water on opposite sides of the planet. They found little blue balls of the mineral hematite all over the surface. This mineral only forms when combined with water. It was proof that the planet once had large oceans.

In 2008, a spacecraft named *Phoenix* landed near the north pole during Martian summer. *Phoenix* was a truly international mission. The effort was a partnership among universities in the United States, Canada, Switzerland, Denmark, Germany and the United Kingdom, as well as NASA, the Canadian Space Agency, and the Finnish Meteorological Institute.

The polar ice caps on Mars are made from a mixture of dry ice (frozen carbon dioxide) and water ice. *Phoenix* searched for life and the water that life needs. It met the second goal right away. As it landed, it blew dust and dirt every which way. Looking down with a camera, scientists saw that *Phoenix*'s engine had uncovered a layer of water ice!

Phoenix never found any life. However, it did show that if the water below the ground was heated, life could survive there.

MRO AND HIRISE

In 2006, Mars Reconnaissance Orbiter (MRO) joined the group of ships orbiting Mars. Its main mission is to study the land, weather and ice of Mars. On board MRO is the HiRISE camera. HiRISE stands for High Resolution Imaging Science Experiment. It is the most powerful camera ever to be sent into deep space.

The camera is so powerful that it can take pictures of things that are smaller than a meter across from over 300 kilometers away. HiRISE has even taken pictures of other ships on the ground.

HiRISE has also found many more water lines on the sides of craters and slopes. It also showed that the water has salt in it, which allows the water to stay liquid for a time in Mars' thin air. HiRISE also took very clear pictures of Mount Sharp and Gale Crater. That was where the Curiosity rover landed in August 2012.

CURIOSITY

NASA's Curiosity rover is the largest vehicle ever to land on Mars. It is bigger than a car, but smaller than a bus. It also has many tools, and it works like a chemistry lab on Mars.

Landing Curiosity was very difficult. It was a process that engineers called "seven minutes of terror." When it got to Mars, it entered the air behind a heat shield. After it slowed down, a parachute slowed it down even more. Once it got closer to the ground, Curiosity was lowered from a device called a "sky crane" on a series of ropes. The parachute was then let go, and rockets on the sky crane slowed it all down more. When Curiosity was set down to the surface, the ropes were cut automatically, and the sky crane flew off to crash land a long way from Curiosity.

It took seven minutes for this whole thing to happen, but nine minutes for the radio signals to reach Earth from Mars. By the time controllers on Earth got the full story, it was all over!

Curiosity was named in an essay contest. The winning entry was sent in by a 12-year-old girl named Clara Ma. She was a sixth-grade student from Kansas. Here is what she wrote:

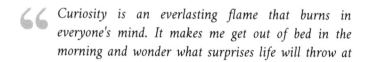 *Curiosity is an everlasting flame that burns in everyone's mind. It makes me get out of bed in the morning and wonder what surprises life will throw at*

me that day. Curiosity is such a powerful force. Without it, we wouldn't be who we are today. Curiosity is the passion that drives us through our everyday lives. We have become explorers and scientists with our need to ask questions and to wonder.

For winning the contest, Ma got to sign her name directly on the spaceship!

The Curiosity rover found evidence of liquid water all over Gale Crater. Just weeks after landing, it sent back pictures of rounded pebbles and worn rocks. These rocks are just like what you would see on river bottoms on Earth. The rocks proved that Gale Crater once had streams and lakes.

Curiosity also sent back pictures of worn layers on the side of Mount Sharp. It spent years traveling toward the mountain and then climbing its steep sides. To steer it, engineers on Earth had to take stereo pictures of Curiosity's path. They studied these pictures and told the rover where to go next.

Nowadays the computer on board Curiosity often makes its own decisions. It takes anywhere from nine to 15 minutes to send commands from Earth to Curiosity. Most of the time, it can see where it is going better than controllers on Earth. The computer on board can decide not to follow instructions from Earth if it senses danger. Then it sends a message back to Earth to tell the humans to pick a different route.

Among Curiosity's many tools is a laser and camera called ChemCam. The laser is shot at a rock, turning its target into gas. ChemCam then takes a look at that gas and can tell what chemicals are in the rock. Sometimes, Curiosity's computer can choose interesting ChemCam targets all on its own, even some as far as seven meters away.

MAVEN, MOM, AND EXOMARS

More countries than ever are exploring Mars. Europe and Russia's ExoMars and the American MAVEN ship are studying Mars' air and gasses. MAVEN and ExoMars have found out how Mars lost its air. Earth is surrounded by an electromagnetic field that keeps the Sun's gasses from hitting the air. Mars does not have the same thing. Over time, this wind of gas from the Sun slowly took more and more of the top layers of Mars' air away. Now, Mars has very little air left.

India also has a ship at the Red Planet. It is called the Mars Orbiter Mission (MOM). It is also called Mangalyaan, which in Sanskrit means "Mars craft." This is India's first ever time to send a ship to another planet, and India has become the first Asian nation to go to Mars. It's also the first country to be successful on its first try.

REFLECTION

1. Why do so many countries want to send missions to Mars?
2. What does Curiosity's ability to "make decisions" on Mars teach us about the future of robots?

9

MARS IN OUR FUTURE

OVERVIEW

No human has been to Mars yet. However, it may be the first planet we visit. The United States made it a goal to send people to Mars since as far back as the 1960s. But the dream of going to Mars goes back even further than that. If current designs succeed, the first person to walk on Mars has already been born!

Wernher von Braun, the man who designed the rocket that sent people to the Moon, also wrote a plan in the 1950s to send people to Mars. Von Braun's plan called for a very large ship that could carry up to 20 people. Once there, they would land near the North Pole because they did not want to interfere with possible plant life. These people would bring an airplane and many roving vehicles. From there, they would go on to live and work on the Red Planet.

Since that time, there have been other plans to send humans to Mars, and many people think it will happen in our lifetime.

THE NEAR FUTURE

Most experts say sending people to Mars will not happen for a long time. However, that does not mean people are not exploring Mars. There are seven missions planned for the next two launch windows when Earth and Mars will be closest.

These plans will involve more nations exploring Mars than ever before. Five different countries, the European Space Agency and a private company all hope to send robot visitors to the Red Planet.

In 2018, NASA plans to send the InSight lander to Mars. It was supposed to go there in 2016, but when an instrument on board failed before launch, engineers changed the schedule. It will be the only ship to head to Mars in 2018.

2020

In 2020, humans plan to send many ships to Mars. Both China and the United Arab Emirates hope to send their first ever ships to the Red Planet. The UAE plan will be the first Mars mission ever sent from an Arab or Muslim nation. The UAE only created their space agency in 2014, and Mars is their first focus. The ship will be named Al Amal, or "Hope." It will be designed and managed entirely by engineers and scientists from their country.

Al Amal is being built to study Mars's atmosphere. It will also help engineers and scientists in the country gain experience and knowledge in learning how to run a space mission. Al Amal is expected to arrive at Mars in 2021. That is also the 50th anniversary of the country.

China also hopes to send its first ship into deep space that year. The Chinese plan is very bold. They hope to send a mission very much like Viking and Pathfinder. The first part of the ship will go around the planet and stay. That ship will also carry a lander, and on board the lander will be a roving vehicle.

The European Space Agency and Russia are partners in the ExoMars lander. This is set to launch from Kazakhstan in July of 2020. The ExoMars lander is designed to find out if life ever existed on Mars. It will also try to find out if life exists there now. Europe and Russia's ExoMars orbiter ship is already there, and it will transmit the lander's signals to Earth.

Also in 2020, SpaceX hopes to become the first private company to send a machine to another planet. The company first planned to send its Red Dragon space ship in the 2020s. It was intended to prepare the planet for future human missions. In mid-2017, SpaceX said it would no longer use the Red Dragon design. Instead, company founder and owner Elon Musk decided the company would build a much bigger ship. Now SpaceX is working on a different landing plan using parachutes instead of engines. Like with all new technologies, SpaceX will probably go through many different changes before settling on a plan they think will work best.

Red Dragon was an ambitious plan. It is also an example of how what is planned and what happens are sometimes very different things.

NASA also plans to send a roving vehicle to Mars in 2020. The vehicle is called Mars 2020. It will look like the Curiosity rover but carry different instruments. Mars 2020 will be designed to look for water and either past or present life on Mars. Like Curiosity, it will also study the geology of the Red Planet.

India's Mangalyaan 2 will visit Mars in the 2020s as well. It may also carry a lander and roving vehicle.

HUMANS TO MARS

Since Mariner 4 in 1964, humans have explored the planet with robots. But no human has ever visited Mars. That might be about to change.

Humans might go to Mars in the next 15 years. The question is what kind of trip will it be? Some people expect to go there without any hope of coming back. Others want to organize a round trip mission, so astronauts can come return to Earth. This would be like the Apollo moon landings. A third plan is to create a permanent settlement on Mars. Two-way space ships could carry people home to Earth. This last plan would be the most complicated.

Going to Mars is not like going to the Moon. The Apollo ships got to the Moon in three days. They were also back on Earth in less than two weeks. Mars takes several months. Once there, travelers have to wait for another year for the two planets to get close again. Then the trip back to Earth takes another several months. In all, the round trip would take over two years, maybe much longer.

No human has ever been on a space trip for that amount of time. Russian Valery Polyakov has the record of 438 days in a row on board the Mir station, from January 1994 to March 1995. Anyone going to Mars would almost double that number!

There are many problems with being in space for a long time. Here are just a few:

1. Human bones lose strength without gravity. This means they can break easily.
2. The Sun sometimes sends bursts of radiation into space. Any ship would have to have heavy shields to protect the humans inside.
3. Any ships would have to carry fuel, water and food for the trip to Mars, the stay there, and the trip back to Earth. It is possible that people could use resources on Mars. Mars has some water to help create fuel and for drinking. However, it would be a very complicated problem to solve.
4. People on Mars would be on their own. When the two

planets are closest, radio messages take three minutes to go one way. When the planets are farthest away, those same one-way commands take 22 minutes.
5. There is very little air on Mars. It is mostly carbon dioxide, so it is deadly to humans.

FUTURE PLANS

The problems of going to Mars have not stopped exploration. The dream of going there is very much alive.

SpaceX owner Elon Musk has said the company plans to send humans around Mars as early as 2024. This would be a very daring mission. Musk has said his ultimate dream is to have SpaceX create a permanent Mars colony. He also claims SpaceX will be able to do this by spending less money than governments.

The private company Mars One also hopes to create a colony on the Red Planet. However, Mars One does not plan to bring anyone back to Earth. This is very controversial. Mars One originally hoped to send people in 2024. However, they have had financial trouble, so their plans have slipped to 2031.

NASA also hopes to send people to Mars in the 2030s. The agency has an idea to create a space station near the Moon called the Deep Space Gateway. At this station, travelers to Mars would prepare for the trip. A ship called the Deep Space Transport would leave from the Deep Space Gateway. This ship could carry people to Mars or other destinations.

China has also announced plans to send people to Mars in the 2030s. Russia plans to send people in the 2040s. If all of this happens, there could be many people living on Mars by the middle of the century.

WHY?

In the future, humans might become a multi-planet species. For years, people have dreamed of making Mars more like Earth, a plan called "terraforming." Many people, including Elon Musk, have said that humans have to live on more than one planet in order to survive.

Studying other planets helps us to understand Earth. For example, when the Mariner 2 ship flew by Venus in 1962, scientists saw that the planet was much hotter than they thought. They quickly learned that this was because the Sun's heat was reaching the planet's surface, but not coming back out.

Venus is like a greenhouse that can never cool down. This helped scientists see that the same thing could happen on Earth.

Studying Mars can bring similar results. Scientists have many questions about how Mars became the way it is today. Getting those answers would help us learn about how all planets work, especially Earth.

William Anders, one of the first men to go to the Moon, once said, "We came all this way to explore the Moon, and the most important thing is that we discovered the Earth." Going to Mars would mean the same thing.

REFLECTION

1. Some people may volunteer to go to Mars without a way back to Earth. Should we let them?
2. Should humans continue to look for earth-like planets and possible life in space? Why or why not?

ABOUT THE AUTHOR

Martin Hajovsky grew up in "Space City" Houston, Texas. He still remembers staring at the Moon as a boy during the Apollo 16 mission. He thought he almost, but not quite, saw people walking around up there.

ABOUT THE SERIES EDITOR

Alice Savage is the series editor for the *Big Ideas* readers as well as the author of several volumes.

Alice has 20 years of experience developing English language learning materials. Whether authoring or working with other writers, her goal is always the same: How can we make English learning easier and more interesting?

54094351R00056

Made in the USA
San Bernardino, CA
07 October 2017